Feeling Blue

Trevor Todd, words
Mark Eatwell, images

MR. WREN WAS FEELING BLUE.

THAT MEANS HE WAS FEELING SAD.

'WHAT'S WRONG?' ASKED MRS. WREN.
'YOU LOOK VERY, VERY SAD TODAY.'

'I CAN'T HELP IT!' HE SULKED.

'TALK TO ME,' SAID MRS WREN,
'SO WE CAN WORK OUT WHY
YOU ARE FEELING BLUE.'

'Sorry,' sighed Mr Wren. 'But I'd much rather sit quietly on a branch by myself.'

MRS. WREN FLEW OVER TO HIM.

'I WANT TO HELP YOU
FEEL HAPPY AGAIN.'

'WELL...' SIGHED MR. WREN....

'IT'S LIKE THIS.'

'I CAN'T LAUGH LIKE KOOKABURRA.'

'I HAVEN'T GOT A BIG SHARP BEAK LIKE MAGPIE.'

'I'M NOT WISE, LIKE OWL.'

'I HAVEN'T GOT A
BRIGHT RED TAIL LIKE
BLACK COCKATOO.'

'Or a bright red chest like Scarlet Robin.'

'AND I CAN'T SOAR UP HIGH
IN THE SKY LIKE EAGLE.'

'IS THAT **ALL**, MY DEAR?' ASKED MRS. WREN.

MR. WREN FLAPPED HIS WINGS AND NODDED.

'Well then... I think I might be able
to help you,' she said,
cuddling up close to him.

She hopped to another branch and said,
'You told me all the things you haven't got.
But what about the things you have?'

'SUCH AS, WE HAVE THREE WONDERFUL CHICKS.'

'AND YOU ARE A VERY KIND DAD.'

'WE HAVE THIS BEAUTIFUL FOREST TO LIVE IN.'

'AND WE HAVE LOTS AND LOTS
OF TASTY GRUBS AND INSECTS TO EAT.'

'*I* ONLY HAVE THESE DULL GREY FEATHERS,
BUT *YOU* HAVE THE MOST *BEAUTIFUL* BLUE FEATHERS
OF ALL THE BIRDS WE KNOW.'

'AND DO YOU KNOW WHAT DAY IT IS?' SHE ASKED.
MR. WREN SHOOK HIS BLUE HEAD. 'NO,' HE REPLIED.

'IT'S WRENSDAY! SO LET'S BE HAPPY AND GRATEFUL FOR THE BEAUTIFUL WORLD WE LIVE IN, AND ALL THE THINGS THAT WE HAVE!'

WITH THAT, MR. WREN CHEERED UP AND
WENT TO FIND SOME TASTY INSECTS
TO FEED TO THEIR CHIRPING CHICKS.

Kookaburra, Magpie, Scarlet Robin, Owl, and Black Cockatoo were as pleased as pleased could be to see that Splendid Blue Wren was happy once again.

IP Kidz

an imprint of IP (Interactive Publications Pty Ltd)
Treetop Studio • 9 Kuhler Court
Carindale, Queensland, Australia 4152
ipoz.biz/ipstore

First published by IP in 2021

A catalogue record for this book is available from the National Library of Australia

Printed in 30 Haarlem Deco ISBN 9781922332721(HB); ISBN 9781922332738 (eBook)

With a feature film, sixteen half hours of television drama, and fourteen books to his credit, **Trevor Todd's** work has reached millions of people worldwide. *Devil's Gate*, a psychological thriller feature film which he co-wrote, was filmed in Scotland and starred Laura Fraser. His *Glad Rags*, a 13 part children's television series, was broadcast on the BBC, Nickelodeon UK and on the Nine Network in Australia.

In 1994 he won the Australian Writers Guild AWGIE for Best Children's Television Drama with *Old Sam, Jasper And Mr Frank*, which was also published by Penguin. In 1996 he took up an Australian Film Commission Creative Nation Fellowship and traveled to Britain to work at Pinewood Studios. He was a guest speaker at the Second World Summit on Television for Children in London in 1998. His books have been translated into Japanese, Korean and Danish.

Trevor is married to psychotherapist and writer, Katie Eden Todd, to whom this book is dedicated, and they live in Western Australia. When not writing he enjoys playing his guitar and singing old Beatles' songs.

Mark Eatwell first started taking photos in Bedfordale, Western Australia several years ago. He was enjoying the local bushland on his walks, and began to share photos of the beautiful wildlife he saw on Facebook. Mark first spotted Old Blue, who is on the cover of this book, in 2016. Since then, he has spent hours photographing Old Blue and his family. He has watched their chicks play games and nestle together to keep warm in winter. He has seen the male chicks mature to develop their bright blue plumage, and leave the nest to start their own families.

Mark's photos and videos have been shared worldwide. The Bedfordale Bush Market and BirdLife Australia have included his photos in their calendars. The City of Armadale has used Mark's photos in their promotional materials, and his photos have appeared in *Aviary Life*, and on several Facebook pages for the Australian Broadcasting Corporation and the *Australian Geographic*. He dedicates this book to his wife Gillian, his daughter Katherine, and of course Old Blue, for being a good friend.

www.ingramcontent.com/pod-product-compliance
Lightning Source LLC
Chambersburg PA
CBHW041600260326
41914CB00011B/1335